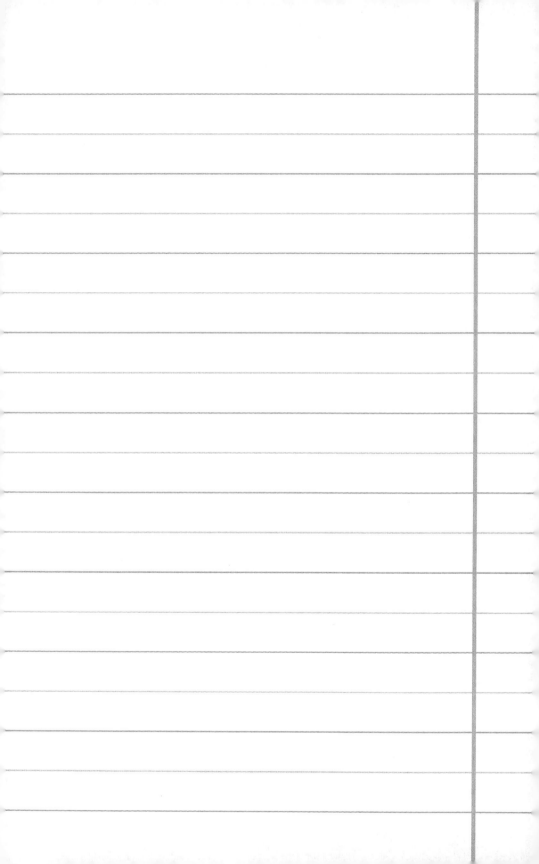

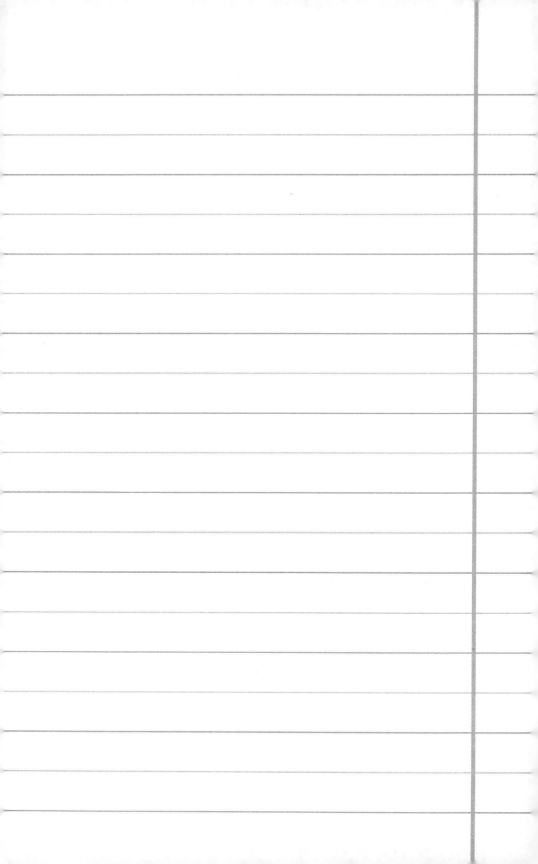

Made in the USA
Middletown, DE
17 August 2019

poetry   you have to

lean into it   give it your softest voice
    your most attentive ear
listen to silences   hear unspoken
  but implied words   pull it like a lover
  against your chest   cup it gently
tenderly in one hand   lift it
   always lift it   revel in the ins and
outs of breaths as it is read
  it whispers from the corner of a dark room
    calls your name in a bad dream   it
gives as all else takes   sleeps within
   you   keeps company through the
most unimaginable of grief   poetry
   you can lean against it
It won't push away
   offers an embrace   comfort   it
envelopes   cushions   changes emotion
  charged yet gentle   poetry   you have
to give it your all   it wants for nothing
   leaves you intact   makes you complete

jazz sex soup

seeking jazz sex soup
as Ginsburg states it
there isn't much else
all attempts at life
where love licks
overlaps into each brass
bed and bowl
an endless search for
a fill up of the soul
disguised as hunger
an insatiable lust
absorbed through senses
that distinguish two
over four legs
appreciation made up
memories flavored by
faded firing neurons
lick the hand that feeds
wag the tail eyes plead
crawl away please
until the next
set lust hunger
filled with desire
mistaken for
music love full belly

vein within

if i trace the vein
of you within myself
will i find over time
that fragile goodbye
in love making shall
hold breath of us
forever
would touch
of you last long
enough to erase
this plague
upon my heart
for all shall leave
for all depart
would memories of
embrace make
this transition
of time and space
easier to bear
i can not answer
this i swear
meeting and parting
your voice your touch
bring back memories
of a time when i was young
dared to dream
lived in hope
knowing i'll awaken
to find you gone
i'd love to hold
be held
one last time

a thunder

crossed the horizon
at daybreak
like ink to paper
before the deluge
that deluded her
made her think of
another time
a time before
this lover

when fear cowered
just under cover
choked the passion
from her loins
soaked sheets like blood
drained her existence
left sweaty stains
smelled of lost causes

she wraps thighs
sticky with life's juices
around the man she loves
allows thunder from
above to guide
love trickle as
he traces her scars
in broad daylight

falling feather

the feather didn't fall
into the snow last night.
it took up residence
like a bomb exploding
in a distant land.
echoes of a
differentiated contrast.
black on white,
violent red on lily.
a nestling place,
a soft place to fall.
catching a crystalized
breath among melting
snow tears.
longing to float,
free and cleansed,
light as a newborn soul.

desire

knees bent
hills behind
sun sets
you recline
against haunches
I lean in
hair dangles loins
tongue licks
laps from ocean
waves overheard
seagulls circle
wide eyed wonder
god approves our
every move
no need for shame
no one to blame
passion has a name
for such
we met
we felt
we live
we fade away

eucalyptus tree

menthol adrift
water lily
entanglement
bull frog
bass tone
drone upon
a magical throne
ebb and flow
moon's first glow
reflects upon water
paddle boats
kayak afloat
we come
we go
adrift then flow
movement
silence

adrift

she walks
shorelines
alone
he and I share
breath   space
move muscled
legs in unison
I take a picture
of him   he of me
later I observe my
eyes squinting, not
from sun reflected
off water's sheen,
rather pain.

she hollers, "you're so relaxed,"
as I try to breathe.

entangled lives paddle the lake.

days later
I know she wishes
to be with him
he with her
all the while
I wish to walk alone
between shore and lily pad
until I find an inner peace
I know is slowly drifting
toward me.

focus

in and out of focus like
leaf   lily pad   touch of
breeze dries tears from cheek
  moment by moment   life unfurls
makes itself known through nature
    billowing cloud   puffs   tugs
movement through time   space
closer   ever closer to you   presence
surrounds   envelopes your essence
warm   moist upon neck   artery
sustain each shallow breath a little longer
birds do it   crickets and horned toads too
this is life   feel it   allow   it won't
last long   there'll always be a time to go
rejoice knowing all   feel   hear   sing
rhythmic life pulses allow them to
reverberate through your flesh   there will
come a time   to   let go   for now
just be

for he who lies

within the box
dreaming of things
left undone, the beauty
of life, a tale homespun,
death comes to all, look
not down, but all around.
it is through death that
life abounds.

haiku

tufted thrush tweets loud/sweet
snow blankets soft down of spring
nest squirms with movement

for each soul's passing
a colorful leaf shall fall
spring brings new formed buds

child's face, crinkled smile
a father's forearm reaching
portrait of childhood

wind upon our back
prairie grass under our feet
sun upon our faces

winter solstice bliss
say goodbye, a final kiss
stark lunar eclipse

Full Moon

Man in the Moon

It was the night his father sat next to him in his
Chevy pickup truck and told him how stupid he was
and how he would never amount to anything.
At first I laughed because I thought his dad was
joking, didn't he have to be joking? But my
giggles didn't change what was being said
or his reaction to his father's words.

Later that night, when we were alone, he told
me to look at the man in the moon. I'd never
noticed the eyes, nose and cheery smile, in
spite of the pock marked face, before. I was
excited to finally see it – that moon face smiling
down on me – and now I can't help but see it.

It's the type of thing, rather like understanding
why someone is so insecure they don't try to
kiss you and don't say goodbye before they leave
town the next morning, that you never forget.

He left his bike on my front porch with
a note saying he loved me and giving
me permission to ride it until he returned.

He never did return, but I think of him,
even though I can't remember his name
and I never learned how to ride a bike.

The man in the moon is a constant reminder
of who the two of us might have been, if
he had not been so worthless and stupid.

Camel Coat

I don my recently dyed, twice retired,
rebuilt, retro camel coat. My hands,
rigid from cold, neck pressed warm
against cloth once fashionably puke green.
Ears like TV antennas are alert for
sounds of sandy crunch on cement steps.
The ones that made the flats
of my palms and knees bleed
when I tripped over my own
damn feet, shoelace untied.
There was no pride in that
humbling free fall. My awkward
stance sucked all thoughts of
romance like paint needed to
repair the rusted white lattice rail he
used to scale. I listen, watch, wait,
impatience my best known trait.
I'm too cold to move, and I'm
counting on a full moon tonight.

Weighing

There were times she thought of going back
to her stalker. After all, when had she felt
so cared for, so loved? She knew that her
life, as she now knew it, her freedom, would end.

He was an amazing lover, possessing her
completely, several times nightly. She was
a sexual person. He didn't allow her to
move during sex. He'd put on an art house
movie, ply her with malted milk balls and
popcorn, they liked lime flavored, while
he massaged her, told her he
loved her as he possessed her. Most
of the time she didn't mind; sometimes
her thoughts alternated between feeling
maternal or that he was a leech
draining her essence.

He was a tech guy who knew
things about putting a book together,
blogging, things that were important
in her love of writing, to know – or to
know someone who could help her learn.

He could be her editor, and she, in her final
seclusion, like a butterfly pinned to the
mat, could write until her wings no longer
desired to unfold or take flight. Where
would she go now anyway?

He had been one of her lovers she'd
told about her MS diagnosis. That
hadn't seemed to bother him. If anything,
his eyes gleamed bright, eager, in

anticipation of the day she would
be wheelchair bound, unable to escape.

She continued to weigh the
pros and cons of a
relationship with him. As
she undressed under the
light of a hazy, weeping,
full moon, she
felt her vagina engorge
with desire. She
watched his shadow
move from one end of
her yard away from
her bedroom window.

A Creative Comeback

After he had his
jaw removed due to
stage four bone cancer, and
part of his shoulder taken
out to refashion a jaw, people
would ask him what had
happened. He'd slowly
pull a handkerchief from a
back pocket of blue jeans,
worn to a flour blue and the
size that would fit a skinny
9 year old boy, wipe the
saliva as it dripped from
his toothless mouth, roll
his eyes, and tell whomever
asked that he'd been
shot in the face by his
lover's angry boyfriend.
It wasn't until several
years after he died
that I realized people
thought I was the
cheating lover.

Our Family

peels potatoes with a knife
rather than a potato peeler.
We sit barefoot at the kitchen table,
sometimes a foot curls under
a leg as the other reaches to a
sister, aunt, grandmother.
Toes point, bony callous on big toe
as much of a family trait as the knife
used for peeling potatoes. A boyfriend
remarks about my feet months
after we've been seeing each other.
My daughter laughs, replies,
"He just now noticed?"
Our family is tall, has white skin,
prone to sunburn, not to wrinkles.
Maybe the peeling skin works to
keep them sloughing off.
Girls have eyes the color of
chromatic brown, a propensity toward
manic depression, boys with blue,
green, hazel eyes, lighter colored hair.
We laugh hard, argue politics,
sexual innuendos flood conversation,
underlying tension brings silence.

Murmuration

My son once said
he felt like one card
in a deck of cards. That
aloneness easily
identifiable to me. I
watch the sky for signs
of God, I see it in the
murmuration of starlings,
schools of pompano.
To feel the surge of
connection, safety of the
group, harmonious
movement, such
promise, such peace.
Susurration,
murmuration....
Omnipresence.
And....me.

Wherever Wind

Why fear when I know which way the wind blows?

Any doubt and I walk from this flat land to stand
under the oldest cottonwood tree, high on the hill,
to feel spit dry upon one finger held skyward.

Which direction will my ashes carry once my
remains no longer matter?

Will they shift and swarm as locusts weathered
during the depression?

Or, if the season is ripe, will they wash through dry
creek beds like the floods survived in the 50s?

Perhaps ashes sift, fine as silt, upon prairie loess
and flowering meadows where bee and bird alike
carry them in all directions.

Or, maybe one blustery day, ashes mix with flakes
so large they cover black earth within seconds,
layering upon frozen ground.

Time no longer a factor.

Fear no longer a presence.

Wherever wind takes me, I remain in Kansas.

Farmers Only

I see your eyes in the
face of a thousand skeletons,
cloaked in the flesh of
strangers as they rattle past in
grocery stores/street corners.
Passengers in cars make
me swivel my head to track,
question, is that you?
Gaunt, haunted, bent forms,
glazed smiles meet my discerning, ever
watchful, eye. I look for you on
farmersonly.com site for
romance even though your olive
hands, with spoon shaped fingers, never
plowed the earth nor milked a cow. I await
your return in hallowed form playing
late night games of mosquito round my
ear; whispering in the voice of
static. The dead pull the strings on
the living's hand jive. I smack a gnat or
moth, wonder if I've killed you. How many
chances will I have to recognize you in
afterlife of buzz and blitz, hum or vibration?
How many chances will I have to love you?

Be... Still

It is here, among the dust, discarded
books, some read, many not, plots
remembered, most forgotten.
It is here, behind the
wall, encased through time,
held by a mind visibly gone
astray with vision blank to
the present, not his presence.
It is here, susurration into the
night, Russian accent,
speech thick, participles
dangle heavy in air,
suspended vibrations of
laughter,
     tears,
       love,
         arguments,
           apologies,
             hellos,
               goodbyes.
It is here, among the rafters,
rattles her breastbone,
light,
   musical,
     harsh,
      scolding.
"Hear me still!" he demands.
"Here, be still," she replies,
pats the warm space next to
herself, drifts asleep to his voice
as it whispers in her ear; her
voice urgent in response.

Passages

Born into a world of bright
filled with round translucent
light, familiar faces surrounding.

Birth of children, red with passion,
the crowning glory of our youth.
Picnics on the ground where
green sprouted out of brown.
Nature supplying seductive,
musical sounds. My frowns
brought laughter as if I
was clown instead of mother.
Love held no boundaries.

Saying goodbye was
an awful resound. An
echoing blackness floated
all around. Shapeless,
it filled spaces left behind.
Memories of a hospital
gown, scents of death still
hound. Years not spent together
wound tight, a stabbing pain.

We thought we'd drown the
summer day we found the
mound to scatter ashes
among his parents' tombs.
Those genes I'd carried in
my womb, knelt beside me,
held my hands.
Beaded blue bled through
like a missing rosary.

I am the Writer

in the woods. With pen and paper
I do purge. I walk through
wind and rain, among small
mammals, over hill and plain.
Solitude my one desire.
Come upon me, utter no words
just smile or bow then go your way.
I'll keep the world at bay today.
No means to speak what it is I think.
Life is eternal when I walk alone.
I spend my time within verse and rhyme
for I am the writer in the woods.

Follow the Call

Flaunt, engage, entice, this plane
I leave behind bliss for one, hell for
another. I'm not turning my back on
you as I go into the wind. I hear your
cries and I will not abandon even
though my shadow no longer lingers
under the roving ways of the sun.

My voice no longer bends in
laughter, echoes with oblique
seagulls or sounding waves upon the
shore. Footprints? None left to
fill. You are as complete as I ever was.

Shouldering the ways of this earthly
experience has brought me to my
knees time and time again,
sometimes broken, more often
to pray. My presence lingers in the
lap of fall, breeze upon your neck,
cloak of rain washes tears away.

I surround and sing as bird upon
highest bough, as swoop and dive of
otter under the surface as he skims.
I'd reach back for you if I could,
knowing you follow brings solace, an
uplifted spirit. Walk on, don't look
back, those who fell off the path
before us, before we felt it was their
time, call loudly. I have no choice but
to follow.

Coats and Friends

I take my coat to you for a remake, It
isn't mine or my mother's. She left
me her wedding dress of dark gray, a
1940s Art Deco mirror, rectangular
shaped with gold swirls on all four
sides, so I can look into my past/future/watch
for her features in my face.
I say, "I'm thinking southwestern style with
horses/silhouettes of birch trees; maybe a sunset."

You say, "If I were to ask you to write a poem for
my wedding, I wouldn't tell you what to write."

I understand it is trust you require
from me, and silence. I respond,
"I wouldn't write a poem about death
for your wedding. I would ask you questions."

I put on the white, wool coat that comes down
to my shins. It is as heavy as a blanket. I think
how lovely it is. Maybe I should leave it
alone. It isn't my mother's coat, but it is
someone's mother's coat. I love it even
though I never wear it.

You say, "Let's shorten it to knee length, add
a couple of buttons here, get rid of the sash."

I picture the new look, think how
modern/light it will feel. You say,
"I'm thinking Art Deco."

I say, "I trust you, and I leave."

Cultural Sisters

Thirty-five years ago and counting,
    who is counting,
we lived on the same street, walked
similar paths and breathed the same
air. Yours was filled with incense that
a neighbor said was to cover the smell
of pot you smoked. That made me
laugh and wish to get to know you even
more. The smell of your food drifted
south, then north, until we converged at
your house, ate food with our fingers
for the first time in our adult lives. I
fell in love with your face, your accent
and ways. Your Rod Stewart hair, strong
personality, unique voice, all so full of
love and acceptance. I was that motherless
child, an orphan grown. You helped me
come into my own. We sang and
danced, shared stories of romance,
divorce, deceased spouse, sister, parent
and niece. We weren't always there to
pick up the pieces. We are now, we
will be tomorrow. We celebrate because
we are different, because we are the
same. We celebrate as sisters having
come full circle on life's path.

A Quiet Man

I snuggle against him watching, 'The
Quiet Man', under the red blanket he
gave his daughter for Christmas. She
isn't here tonight, she's with, 'The
Mother'. That's how he refers to his ex.

I look at him when I think he won't
notice. I see tiny freckles on his skin.
They make him look somehow
fragile, but even more handsome.
All the years I've known him
professionally, I've never noticed
them before, but I wasn't snuggled
under a red blanket with him then.

I've told him once how much I love
him, the night of our first date, that
I've loved him for decades, that it's
my turn to be with him, that
I've been patient.

He replied, "Oh my!" the way he
now does when I touch him a certain
way when we make love.

For now, I wait. I hold the words
inside to keep them safe. I won't say
them to anyone else. I'll say them to
him one day, after he says
them to me.

One Slip Up

He flirts with me, I
ignore him until my
usual mode of operation,
until I need something.

It isn't as though I have
to resort to that technique.
It isn't as though I'm not
capable of asking or doing
things myself. But old
habits die hard, especially
when one becomes displaced
from home, taken decades
into the past where I once
lived, once rode the
school bus with him.

He gives me his phone
number, suggests he has a
story of interest from the
old days I might enjoy. I
don't remember him until
he clarifies his name was
Jerry then, not Gerome.

Decades past, we rode on
the yellow school bus that
arrived much too early. My
older sister and I were
picked up first which made
for an hour's ride both
mornings and afternoons.

We were on that bus
long enough to do homework,
catch up on friends' social
lives, learn about life, be
told our paternal grandfather
had died, and, of course, get
into trouble.

Always curious, I sent
'Gerome' a text. He replied
I'd worn a mini dress one
day. When he informed
me he could see my slip, my
response, he said, was to
hike my dress higher.

All the things I've
accomplished in my life
come down to a past
moment in this assisted
living place, where I spend
time waiting for an uncle to
die, assist an aunt to continue
living. A lasting connection
because of one slip up.

Morning Dove Aviso

First light I hear
your mournful cry. In
and of itself that's
not meaningful,
since each
morning I listen for
your sound upon
waking. Because
it draws extra attention, I
watch for signs post song.

Mid morning an email from
my ex, decades since
gone, comes to convey a
friend has passed. Your
song, dear amigo, an
aviso to hold my
heart in my hands, to
allow tears to flow. Their
saltiness a delicious
taste upon my pallet.

Lite House

I shared with you from our first
moments dreams of capsized
boats, drowning, water washing
me ashore. I didn't know until
the telling what they meant.

Looking into your eyes, hearing
your story of encroaching death, I
knew I was flooding, not from
without, regardless of metaphor
or vessel, but from within.

Our first meeting hugs, tears,
a knowledge of unspoken,
unspeakable shared grief. I
held you as lighthouse, beacon,
revered mentor. You touched my
tears, overlooked my fragility,
allowed me to lean against
you, even though I, physically,
was stronger than you.

And as this, your end, draws near,
you reach through space with
strength I do not have. You touch
me one last time to share words
of praise, knowing how important
goodbyes are for mooring, and
just how lost I am at sea.

Tell God Hi

for me I joke as he lists a kiss to
my lips and walks out the door
on his way to Sunday school.

I stay in bed propped
against a pillow and heating
pad. I fell on the snow slippery
driveway yesterday.

My commune will be the spirituality
I find in poems I edit for a favorite
poet from Wichita. Both my lover
and the poet were raised Catholic.
I wonder how different my
spirituality might be had it
been the same for me.

Movement outside the window
draws my eyes upward to view a
squirrel on the neighbor's roof
doing a downhill slalom
ski move around the chimney.

I think of poetry, where it takes me;
how it soothes and heals,
invigorates, connects me to
humankind, here and now,
for eternity.

I think of turning onto my side the
night before; the feel of his warm
belly spooned against my back, legs
curved, feet entwined. That afterglow
as natural, as fulfilling, as poetry.

Nor' Easter

Nor' easterly I go, if not
through rain then snow.

Follow the river with
mud caked shoes.

Remember, it twists and
turns then rights itself again.

I trust the path and
love the plains. The
hills are steep. With life
comes trials, I ascertain.

I judge not the journey
for I know, it's how I
remain in touch with
who I am and how I grow.

This lone wanderer loves
the land and sky so much.

They lead me not
astray, but by day's
end, so shall my journey,
then I'll be home again.

Meeting Noah

I met Noah today. He rests
along a road I'd never been
down. Two dinosaurs adorn the
front of his headstone.

He was four days old when he
died; these days, he would be
nine years old. We plant a pink
peony, his dad and I. He digs
up a large spade full of grass; I
hold the plant still as he gently
places one shovelful of moist,
damp earth after another
over its bare roots.

I listen to the circumstances of
Noah's death where a definition
means more than a word –
born with internal organs on
the outside of the body.
The telling and retelling help
mend an exposed heart.

"He was like a comet flashing across
the sky; here, and then just gone."

I feel as though I've watched Noah
grow up, even though he never went
home. The cross-stitch his father
did of him squatting in the sand on a
beach shows what he may have
looked like at age three. His blond
hair is tousled, blue eyes large,

wide-eyed, in wonder of the beauty
of the universe surrounding.

A Chevy truck breaks our silence
as it goes slowly past the cemetery
turn off. We see Noah's younger
brother and sister, faces pressed
against the window, inside with
their maternal grandparents.

We wonder out loud what the kids are
saying; if they ask to come to their
dad, what their grandmother replies.

I wonder, silently, if this family of
Noah's, now separated by death and
divorce, will continue to come to this
site several times yearly for
generations. I hope down the lineage,
they will one day stand together.

We head west, Noah's father and
I, where brown earth has rolled
onto her back. Her soft, warm belly,
recently itched and raked by farm
machinery, unashamedly exposed.

I am My Home

though guests are welcome
for a short visit or two,
and when no visitors
come I sometimes feel blue,
I am my home,
I live quite alone,
with all of my favorite things.
With words as my food,
and thoughts as my bed,
I've become comfortable
alone in my head.
I am my home,
I keep house with my heart.

Publication Notes

Some of the poems in this book were previously published in the following publications. A special thank you to those editors who previously published them!

Lawrence Journal World: Spanish Moss - 6/26/2010, Cultural Sisters - 12/08/2013, Tell God Hi - 2/16/2014, Unspoken Bonds - 9/07/2014, Nor' Easter - 2/15/2015, Good Night, My Friends, Good Night - 03/29/2011, Charlie - 04/26/2015

BEGIN AGAIN: 150 Kansas Poems, Caryn Mirriam-Goldberg, Editor, 2011, Woodley Memorial Press Topeka, Kansas: Creek Play

Kansas Time + Space Here & Now, Then & There: Winter Witch – 3/31/2014, Coats and Friends – 4/21/2014, MoonStain – 2/15/2015

Poem on the Range: A Poet Laureate's Love Song to Kansas, Caryn Mirriam-Goldberg, 2014, Coal City Press, Lawrence, KS: Creek Play

Tallgrass Voices, Gary Lechliter, Editor, 2011, Hill Song Press, Lawrence, Kansas: Spanish Moss, I am My Home

The Percolator, a project space of the Lawrence Corporation for the Advancement for Visual Arts, Lawrence, KS., - What My Mother Didn't Teach Me - 1/2013

The Shine Journal – The Light Left Behind: Be Still, Wherever Wind, Passages

To the Stars Through Difficulties: A Kansas Renga in 150 Voices," Caryn Mirriam-Goldberg, Editor, 2012, Mammoth Press, Lawrence, KS: Stone Eyed Cold Girl

View from Smoky Hill: MoonStain, Wherever Wind, Winter Witch, What My Mother Didn't Teach Me, Spanish Moss, Stone Eyed Cold Girl, Passages, Lite House, Meeting Noah, Tell God Hi, I am My Home, Follow the Call, Unspoken Bonds, Embrace, Creek Play, Coats and Friends, Barns Don't Die,

Zingara Poetry, http://zingarapoet.net/: Camel Coat - 08/07/2013, Be Still - 04/17/2013

About the Poet

Ronda Miller is a Life Coach who works with clients who have lost someone to homicide. She is a graduate of The University of Kansas and continues to live in Lawrence. She is a Fellow of The Citizen Journalism Academy, World Company, a Certified Life Coach with IPEC (Institute of Professional Empowerment Coaching), mother of Scott and Apollonia. She created poetic forms loku and ukol. She is the current poetry contest manager for Kansas Authors Club (2011 – 2014) as well as the District 2 President. She is the co-chair, along with Caryn Mirriam-Goldberg, for the Transformative Language Arts Conference to be held at Unity Village September, 2015.

Note from Ronda

Events happen in everyone's lives that leave a mark or a stain. For many, it occurs early in life, as it did for me with the loss of my mother. For others, it may happen later.

Stains don't imply a negative; they are, however, life changing. The filter, through which we view ourselves and the world around us, becomes forever changed. These stains, and our perceived view of life, are what make us unique; help give us our own voice.

Specifically, MoonStain describes the blood moon as it shines through tree leaves, marking the long hours of a sleepless night as it spreads from one point to another on a young child's bedroom floor. The child has been stained by her mother's suicide. She is fearful and sees only the negatives on her grandmother's farm: a dead calf, rattlesnake, swarming balls of winged ants. Even the colors she notices, lit by the blood moon, are blood colored - rhubarb, strawberries, ants, and a rusted screen door.

In order to understand the complex and complete person we become, one must examine all of the events that play a role, through stain or illumination, large or small.

Appreciations

Thanks to my family and close friends for their support – it begins and ends there. To all the teachers in my life (Carl Werner, Barbara Ewing, James Gunn, Chester Sullivan) in and out of the classroom, who saw something in my writing long before I did. Ralph Gage of The World Company, and its Citizen Journalism Academy, helped bring about a confidence and freedom in my writing which possibly shouldn't have been allowed, but changed my perception of what I could write – namely poetry! To the fans of my blog, known as The Backyarders, such fun times, night and day! Roger Shimomura for accepting my poem, *Renunciation*, to go with his personal papers to The Smithsonian Art Institute Archives. By doing so, he fed my soul. For my friend and world class photographer, Richard Gwin, for commissioning me to write *The 150th Reride of The Pony Express* documentary. Caryn Mirriam-Goldberg, I thank for her inclusion in anthologies, her friendship, mentoring, and journeys across Kansas, sharing of poetry, Cheetos, her wondrous spirit, and introduction to numerous poets who have become mentors and close friends. These poets are too numerous to mention, but include Roy Beckemeyer, Dan Pohl, Diane Watho, Bill Hagman, Dixie Lubin, Nancy Hubble, Liz Black, Wyatt and Roderick Townley – and the coven of poets in north Lawrence! Kansas Authors Club members embraced me when I most needed an escape into words. Diane Palka, Gordon Kessler, Duane Johnson, Tom Mach, Susie Nightingale, Maryann Barry, Vicki Julian, Annola Charity, Andrew Mitchell, Mike Hartnett, Sally Jadlow and

Lee Goldstein are inspirations unto themselves. Brian Daldorph for being the lifeline he is to so many, and allowing me to go to prison with him! Denise Low, who took time to make me feel worthwhile, has always encouraged me to continue writing, and made suggestions of places to show my manuscript. Beth Schultz I thank for simply being Beth Schultz. Marcia Epstein I thank for her generous spirit, healing of wounds, embracing words, making introductions into new worlds. So many Lawrence poets should be on this list! Special thanks to Megan McHenry, Topher Enneking, Mark Hennessey, and the other performance poets whose brave words encourage me to go deeper. To the wonderful poets who took time to read *MoonStain* in varied stages: Caryn Mirriam-Goldberg, Denise Low, Brian Daldorph, Kevin Rabas, David W. Romtvedt, Xanath Caraza, Kim Stafford (without his request for the poem *MoonStain*, this book wouldn't have come about). Thanks to Meadowlark Books for believing in my poetry. Lastly, my editor, Tracy Million Simmons, who I knew I could trust on so many levels including expertise, professionalism, insight, wisdom, and making *MoonStain* unique and pretty.

Meadowlark is an independent publisher, born of a desire to produce high-quality books for print and electronic delivery. Our goal is to create a network of support for today's independent author. We provide professional book design services, assuring that the stories we love and believe in are presented in a manner that enhances rather than detracts from an author's work.

For all the debate about the state of publishing today, we remain optimistic. Readers continue to seek quality stories and writers have more opportunities than ever before.

We look forward to developing a collection of books that focus on a Midwest regional appeal, via author and/or topic. We are open to working with authors of fiction, non-fiction, poetry, and mixed media. For more information, please visit us online:

www.meadowlark-books.com

Made in the USA
Middletown, DE
17 August 2019